A MODERN METHOD FOR GUITAR

william leavitt

volume 1

Editorial Consultants: Larry Baione and Charles Chapman

Berklee Media

Associate Vice President: Dave Kusek
Director of Content: Debbie Cavalier
Marketing Manager: Jennifer Rassler
Senior Graphic Designer: David Ehlers

Berklee Press

Senior Writer/Editor: Jonathan Feist
Writer/Editor: Susan Gedutis
Product Marketing Manager: David Goldberg
Production Manager: Shawn Girsberger

ISBN 978-0-7935-4511-7

DISTRIBUTED BY

HAL•LEONARD®
CORPORATION
7777 W. BLUEMOUND RD. P.O. BOX 13819
MILWAUKEE, WISCONSIN 53213

1140 Boylston Street
Boston, MA 02215-3693 USA
(617) 747-2146

Visit Berklee Press Online at
www.berkleepress.com

Visit Hal Leonard Online at
www.halleonard.com

Printed in the United States of America.

Contents

It is important that the following material be covered in consecutive order. The index on page 126 is for reference purposes only and will prove valuable for review or concentration on specific techniques.

Section I

Section II

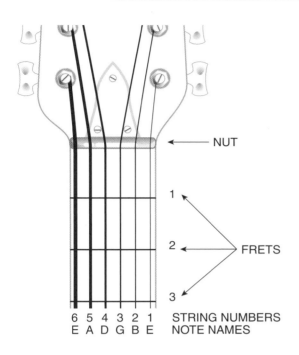

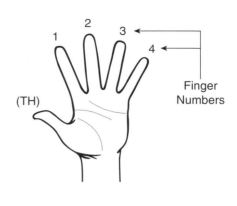

(TH)

Finger
Numbers

NUT

1
2 FRETS
3

6 5 4 3 2 1   STRING NUMBERS
E A D G B E   NOTE NAMES

TO TUNE THE GUITAR: (using piano or pitch pipe)
1. Tune the open 1st string to the first E above middle C.
2. Press the 2nd string down at the fifth fret and tune (2nd string) until it sounds exactly the same as the open 1st string.
3. Press the 3rd string down at the fourth fret and tune (3rd string) until it sounds exactly the same as the open 2nd string.
4. Press the 4th string at the fifth fret and tune to the open 3rd string.
5. Press the 5th string at the fifth fret and tune to the open 4th string
6. Press the 6th string at the fifth fret and tune to the open 5th string

THE STAFF: consists of five lines and four spaces, and is divided into *measures* by *bar lines.*

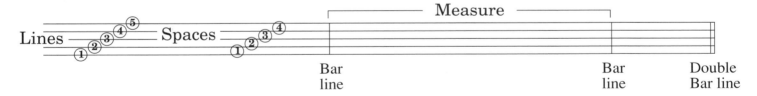

Lines   Spaces   Measure

Bar
line

Bar
line

Double
Bar line

CLEF SIGN: Guitar music is written in the *treble* (or "G") *clef.* The number of sharps (♯) or flats (♭) found next to the clef sign indicate the key signature (to be explained more fully later).

"G" clef shows the
position of the note G

COMMON TIME VALUE OF THE NOTES:

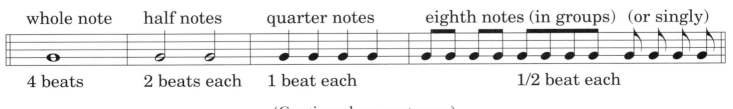

whole note   half notes   quarter notes   eighth notes (in groups) (or singly)

4 beats   2 beats each   1 beat each   1/2 beat each

(Continued on next page)

TIME SIGNATURES: Next to the clef sign (at the beginning of a composition), locate the two numbers (like a fraction) or a symbol that represents these numbers. The top number tells how many beats (or counts) in a measure, and the bottom number indicates what kind of note gets one beat.

EXAMPLE: **4/4** means four quarters, or four beats per measure, with a quarter note receiving one beat or *count*. The symbol is **C** .

Notes in the First Position

No sharps or flats—Key of C major.

Order of the notes going up the scale:
A B C D E F G, A B C D E F G, A B…
Start at any point and read left to right.

■ **EXERCISE 1**

■ Read the *notes,* not the fingering. Fingering numbers will eventually be omitted.

■ **EXERCISE 2**

■ **EXERCISE 3**

■ **EXERCISE 4**

5

Sea to Sea (duet)

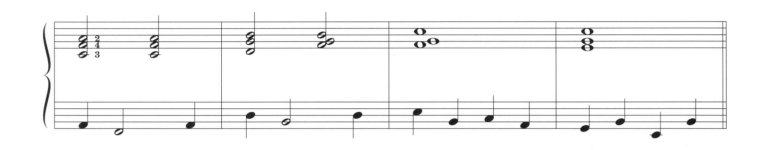

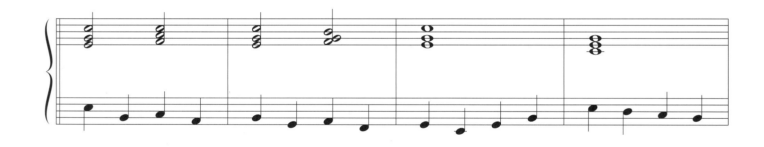

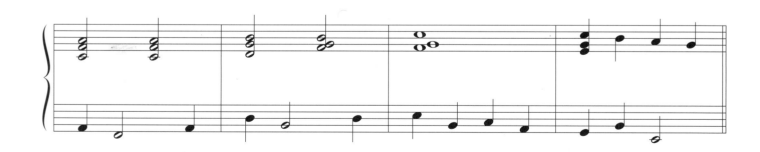

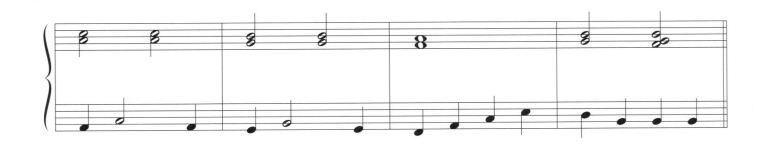

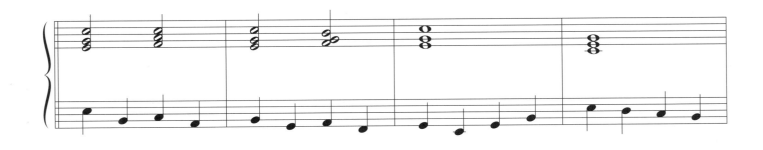

Starting on C one *octave* higher than C found on the 5th string, we complete the *upper register* of the first position.

■ **EXERCISE 5**

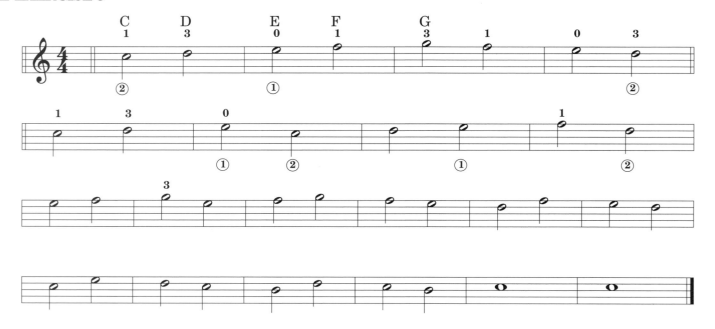

■ **EXERCISE 6**

Note and Chord Review

■ **EXERCISE 7**

■ **EXERCISE 8**

Regular review of all material is a must!

One, Two, Three, Four (duet)

Tempo (Speed): Moderate 4

Rhythm Accompaniment

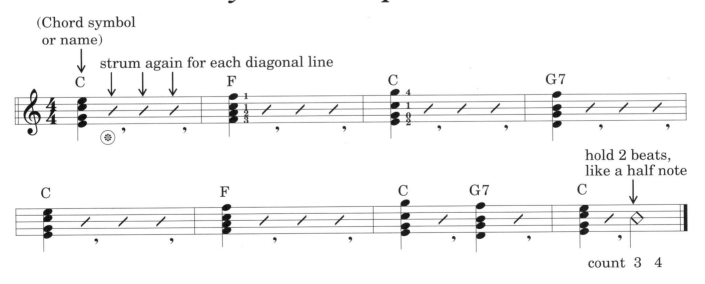

(*) A better rhythmic pulse is produced if you relax left-hand pressure at these points ('). However, do not remove fingers from strings. Also, if open strings are involved, mute them with the side of the right hand at the same instant that you relax left-hand pressure.

■ *Ledger lines* are added below or above the staff for notes too low or too high to appear on the staff.

■ **EXERCISE 9**

Review

Complete first position—Key of C major.

■ **EXERCISE 10**

Imitation Duet

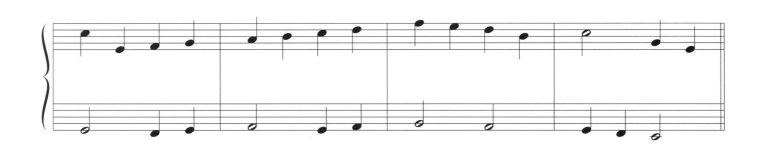

Sharps and Flats

A note that is not altered by a sharp or flat is called *natural*.

▌ A *sharp* (♯) raises the note a half tone (one fret). A *flat* (♭) lowers the note a half tone (one fret).

▌ When a sharp or flat appears in the *key signature* (between the clef sign and the time signature), it is used throughout the entire piece.

▌ When a sharp or flat that is not in the key signature appears in the piece, it is called an *accidental* and is used only for the remainder of that measure. The next bar line cancels it out.

▌ The natural sign (♮) is used to cancel out accidentals within the same measure. It is also used as a reminder that the bar line has cancelled the accidental.

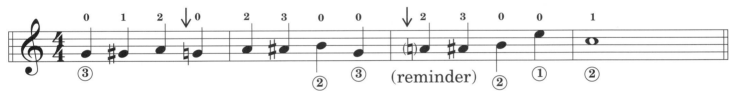

▌ When the natural sign is used to cancel a sharp or flat found in the key signature, cancellation is good only for the remainder of the measure.

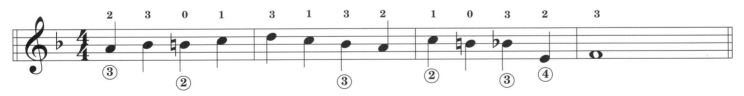

■ **EXERCISE**

15

Here We Go Again (duet)

❋*Mute,* or deaden, the 5th string by lightly touching it with the side of the third finger so it
will not sound.

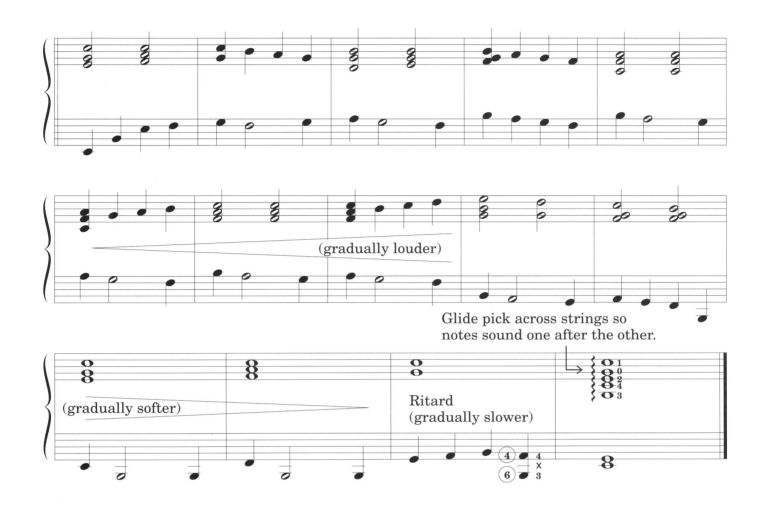

(gradually louder)

Glide pick across strings so
notes sound one after the other.

(gradually softer)

Ritard
(gradually slower)

Rhythm Accompaniment
Bass Notes and Chords

All chord symbols (names) appearing as only a letter are assumed to be *major* chords. A letter followed by the number "7" represents *dominant 7* chords. A letter followed by a small "m" indicates *minor*.

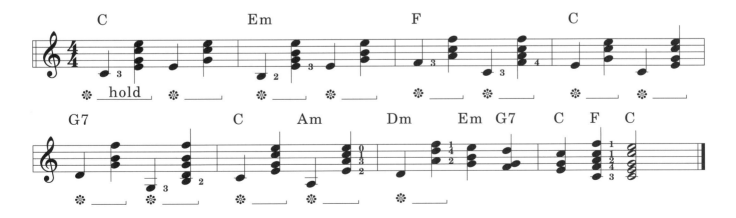

Do not skip or "slight" any lesson material.

Eighth Notes—Counting and Picking

⊓ means "pick downward"   V means "pick upward"

■ EXERCISE 1

count   1   &   2   &   3   &   4   &

count   1   2   &   3   4   &

■ EXERCISE 2

❀ *Fermata* means "hold."

⌒ is a fermata. It indicates to hold the note.

Review of all material is a must.

■ EXERCISE 3

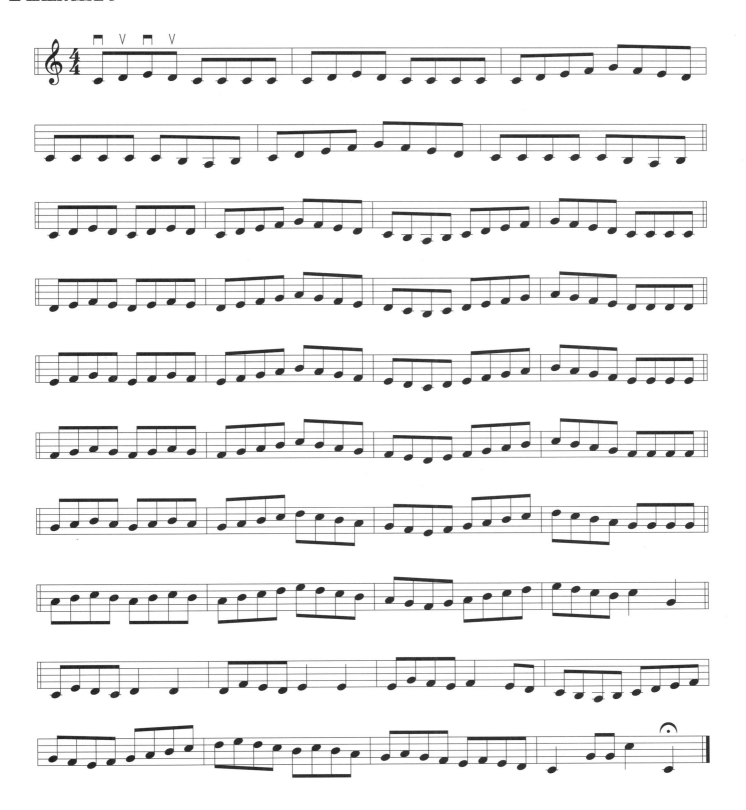

19

Etude No. 1 (duet)

Rests, Tied Notes, Dotted Notes

COMMON TIME VALUES OF RESTS (periods of silence):

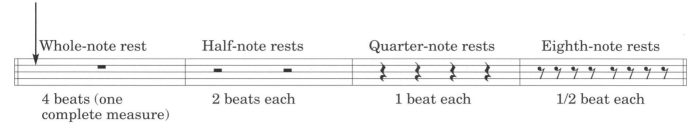

Whole-note rest	Half-note rests	Quarter-note rests	Eighth-note rests
4 beats (one complete measure)	2 beats each	1 beat each	1/2 beat each

TIED NOTES: When two notes are "tied" together with a curved line, only the first note is picked. The second note is merely held and counted.

DOTTED NOTES: A "dot" placed after any note increases the time value of the note by one-half. Or you may say a "dot" found next to any note receives half the time value of the note itself.

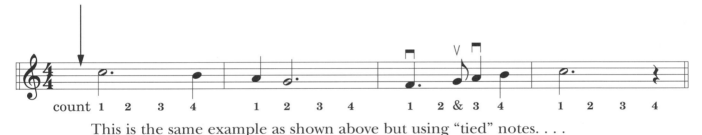

This is the same example as shown above but using "tied" notes. . . .

■ **EXERCISE**

❙ Count aloud as you play.

Etude No. 2 (duet)

First Solo

Solo arrangement: with melody and accompaniment.

Accompaniment chord is
played on the 2nd beat

Melody note is picked on the 1st beat
and held while chord is played

Be sure to hold all notes for their full time values.

Rhythm Accompaniment

CHORD DIAGRAMS

1. Vertical lines represent strings.
2. Horizontal lines represent frets.
   (See illustration, pg. 3.)
3. Dots represent finger placement.
4. Numbers indicate fingers to be used.
5. Zero means open string.
6. × means muted string.

■ EXERCISE 1

▐ Use only the chord forms shown above.

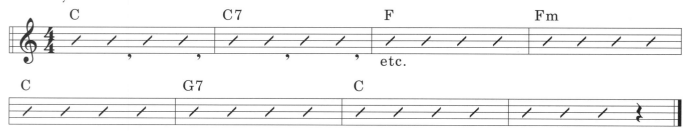

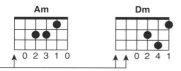

If no number, zero, or × is found below the diagram, do not allow the pick to strike the string

Optional fingered note or open string

■ EXERCISE 2

■ EXERCISE 3

▐ This exercise combines all forms shown above, and should not be attempted until the preceding chord sequences are mastered at least partially.

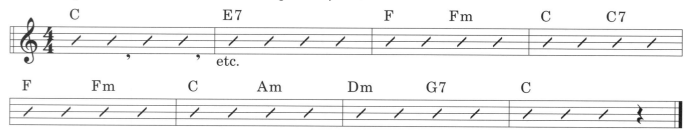

All chord forms must be memorized.

24

Second Solo

Solo arrangement with melody *above* (and *below*) the chord accompaniment.

Hold all notes for their full value.

Etude No. 3 (duet)

count   1   2   3   4   &

count   1   2   3   &   4   &

1   2   &   3   4

Ritard   Fine

Review everything regularly.

Picking Etude No. 1

For development of the right hand.

PREPARATION

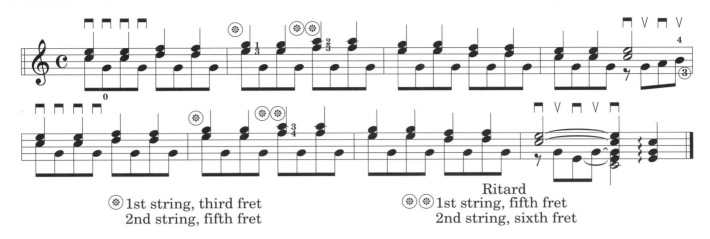

⊛ 1st string, third fret
2nd string, fifth fret

⊛⊛ 1st string, fifth fret
2nd string, sixth fret

Etude

Tempo: Moderately Slow 4

Two, Two (duet)

al coda

1 & 2 &

al coda

3 4 2

count 1 & 2 &

count 1 & ah 2 &

D.S. al coda

D.S. al coda

Play again from
the (𝄋) sign to the
al coda. Then skip
to the coda (⊕).

coda

coda

3 4 2

1
3
2

1
2
0

Fine

Key of G Major (First Position)

(All Fs are sharped.)

Rhythm Accompaniment

G°7(diminished 7)

This chord structure is also indicated by the abbreviation "dim." Even though the numeral 7 is often omitted from the symbol, diminished 7 is intended.

■ EXERCISE 1

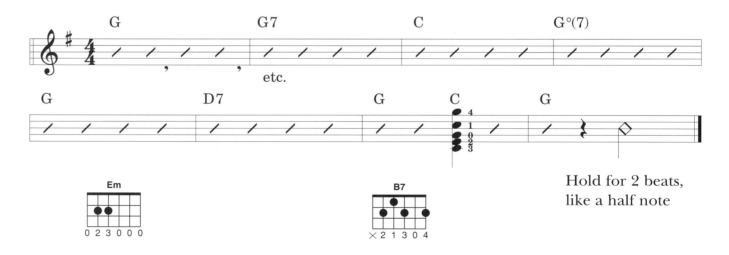

Hold for 2 beats, like a half note

■ EXERCISE 2

■ **EXERCISE 3**

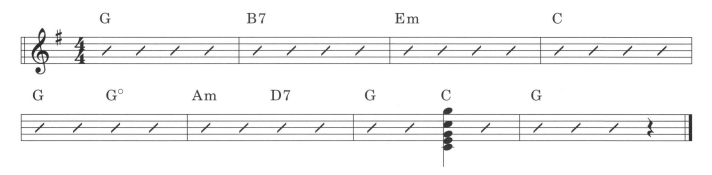

Sixteenth Notes

Duet in G

Fine

Picking Etude No. 2

For alternate picking while skipping strings.

■ Pay very strict attention to "down" and "up" pickings on all eighth-note passages.

Another Duet in G

count   1 & 2 & 3 & 4 &

Ritard   Fine

Key of F Major (First Position)

(All Bs are flatted.)

Rhythm Accompaniment

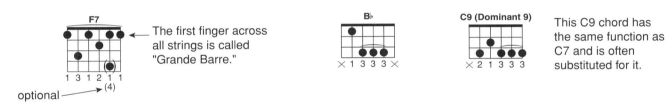

F7 — The first finger across all strings is called "Grande Barre."
1 3 1 2 1 1
optional → (4)

B♭
✕ 1 3 3 3 ✕

C9 (Dominant 9) — This C9 chord has the same function as C7 and is often substituted for it.
✕ 2 1 3 3 3

■ EXERCISE

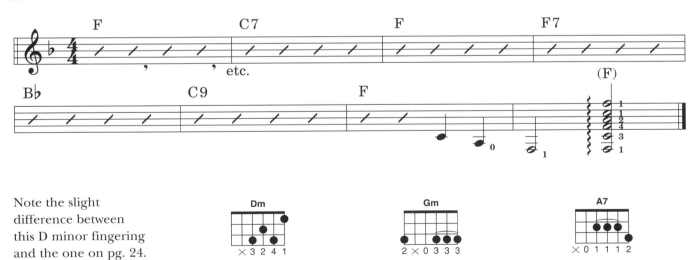

Note the slight difference between this D minor fingering and the one on pg. 24.

Dm
✕ 3 2 4 1

Gm
2 ✕ 0 3 3 3

A7
✕ 0 1 1 1 2

■ EXERCISE

■ Several of the forms presented above will take some time to play clearly. Be patient and keep at them.

Duet in F

The Triplet

There are two ways to pick consecutive sets of triplets. Practice the entire exercise thoroughly, using first the picking marked Type 1. Then practice using Type 2.

■ EXERCISE

Review all material.

Waltz in F (solo)

A waltz has three beats per measure.

Notes appearing before the beginning measure are called *pick-ups*

count 2   3   1   2   3 etc.

Rall. ("Rallentando," or slow down)

A tempo (back in tempo)

Ritard poco a poco (little by little)

Fine

Key of A Minor (First Position)

Relative to C major.

■ The sixth degree (note) of any major scale is the tonic (first note) of its *relative minor key*. The major and relative minor key signatures are the same. There are three different scales in each minor key.

■ A Natural Minor: All notes exactly the same as its relative major, C major.

■ A Harmonic Minor: The 7th degree, counting up from A, is raised a half step.

■ A Melodic Minor: The 6th and 7th degrees are raised *ascending* but return to normal descending.

Rhythm Accompaniment

■ We now begin to observe that many chords have more than one fingering. The choice of which one to use generally depends upon the chord fingerings that immediately precede and/or follow. In the following exercise use the large diagrams *or* the smaller optional fingerings in sequence. Do not mix them!

■ **EXERCISE**

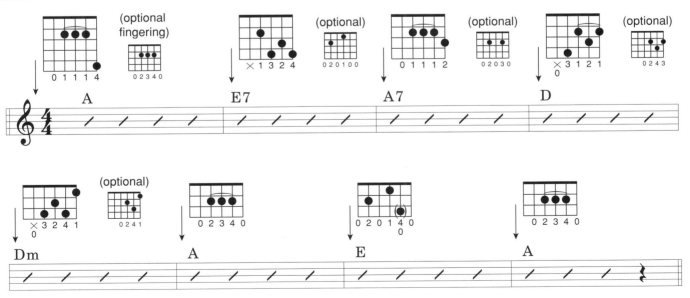

Smooth, melodic accompaniment depends
on the number of chord forms mastered.

Pretty Pickin' (duet)

For alternate picking while skipping strings.

CHORD PREPARATION

Slowly

Fine

Duet

Moderate Waltz Tempo

(All notes under the curved line must be kept ringing.)

Crescendo
(get louder)

Diminuendo
(or get softer)

※ (Repeat from the beginning to the coda)

Dotted Eighth and Sixteenth Notes

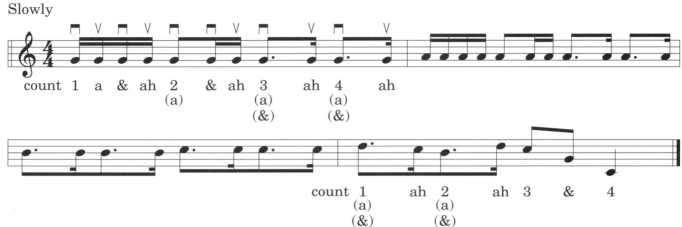

■ **EXERCISE 1**

Slowly

count 1 a & ah 2 & ah 3 ah 4 ah
    (a)   (a)   (a)
    (&)   (&)

count 1   ah 2   ah 3 & 4
   (a)   (a)
   (&)   (&)

■ **EXERCISE 2**

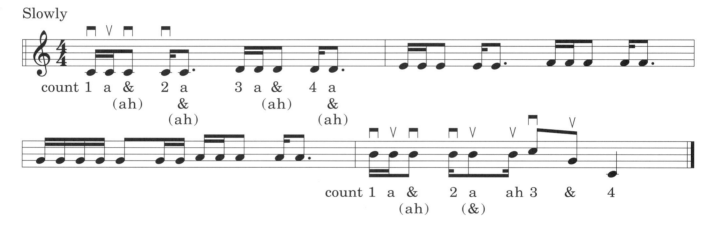

Slowly

count 1 a & 2 a 3 a & 4 a
   (ah)   &   (ah)   &
   (ah)   (ah)   (ah)

count 1 a &   2 a   ah 3 & 4
   (ah)   (&)

Note that the above "strict" (or "legitimate") interpretation of dotted eighth and sixteenth notes produces a rather jerky rhythm. In pop music and jazz they are played more *legato* (smoothly, in a flowing manner). This is done by treating them as triplets.

Example:

■ **EXERCISE 3**

Slowly

count 1 & ah 2 & ah 3   ah 4   ah
     (&)   (&)

(Keep the "3" feeling)

Key of E Minor (Scales in First Position)

Relative to G major.

E Natural Minor

E Harmonic Minor

E Melodic Minor

Rhythm Accompaniment

■ **EXERCISE 1**

(First ending
play first time only)

(Second ending
play second time only)

Fine

■ **EXERCISE 2**

etc

In waltz time, chords are muted immediately after the second and third beats.

Take Your Pick (duet)

For alternate picking while skipping strings.

CHORD PREPARATION

Rhythm Accompaniment

The principle of movable chord forms.

▌ Moving up the fingerboard in pitch, *natural* notes are two frets apart, except E to F, and B to C. They are one fret apart.

EXAMPLE (1st or 6th string)

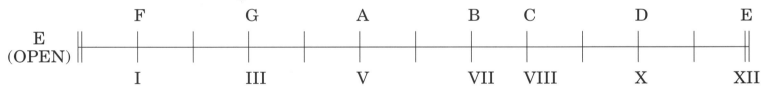

This fact applies to chord playing as follows:

1. If you play F major, F minor, and F7 on the first fret, then (using the same fingering) G major, G minor, and G7 will be on the third fret (two frets above F). Moving still higher, A major, A minor, and A7 will be on the fifth fret, B major, B minor, and B7 on the seventh fret, and C major, C minor, and C7 will be on the eighth—one fret up from B.

2. All *movable* forms will have *no open strings*.

3. Sharps and flats alter chord positions by one fret, the same as single notes.

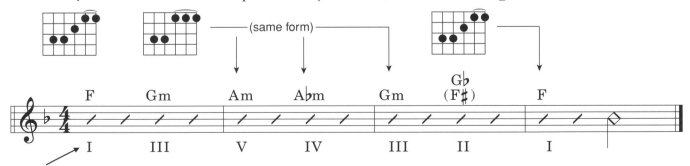

▌ The Roman numerals (called "Position Marks") indicate the frets on which the first finger plays.

▌ On the following pages, all new chord forms will be movable.

Chromatic Scale (First Position)

■ The *chromatic scale* is made up of semi-tones (half steps).

Speed Studies

▌Play the following eighth-note patterns at an even speed, slowly at first. Very gradually (over a period of time), increase the tempo. *Memorize the patterns*, and practice each one in all keys. Always start on the *tonic* (first note) of each scale and *transpose* the rest of the notes by the following pattern. (Write them out if necessary.)

PATTERN 1

PATTERN 2

PATTERN 3

First-position F and G scales can be played in two octaves. Play all patterns in *both* octaves.

Key of D Minor (Scales in First Position)

Relative to F major.

Rhythm Accompaniment

■ **EXERCISE 1**

■ This is the same chord sequence but *transposed* to a different key. Watch the position marks.

■ **EXERCISE 2**

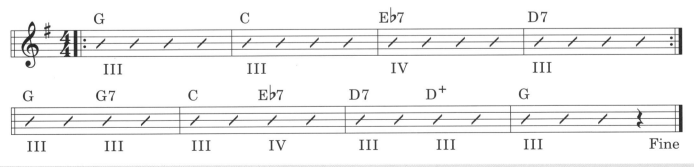

The augmented chord can actually be named from any note within the form (C+ = E+ = G♯+ or A♭+).
Augmented chords repeat themselves every fifth fret.

Endurance Etude
Picking Etude #3

Hold fourth finger down throughout.

Be sure to observe tempo changes. Also, vary the *dynamics* (degrees of volume, loud and soft) to make the music more interesting to listen to.

Key of B♭ Major (Scales in First Position)

(All Bs and Es are flatted.)

When a key signature has two or more flats, the name of the next-to-last flat is the name of the key.

Rhythm Accompaniment

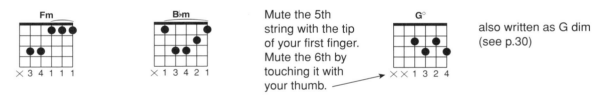

Mute the 5th string with the tip of your first finger. Mute the 6th by touching it with your thumb.

also written as G dim (see p.30)

■ EXERCISE 1

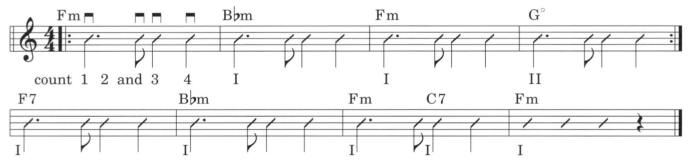

■ EXERCISE 2

This is the same chord sequence but transposed to a different key. Watch the position marks.

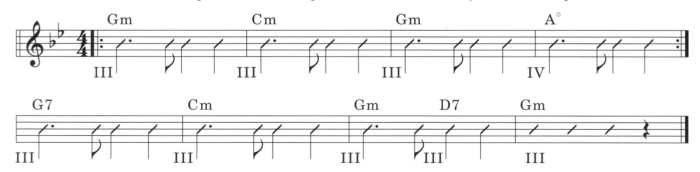

The diminished chord can actually be named from any note in the form (G° = B♭° = C♯° or D♭° = E°).
Diminished chords repeat themselves every fourth fret.

Duet in B♭

(Finger complete chord form. Do not strum top string.)

Reverse Alternate Picking Study

▌ Pay very strict attention to picking as indicated.

(hold down bottom note)

Review all material.

Key of D Major (Scale in First Position)

(All Fs and Cs are sharped.)

In any sharp signature, the first note above
the last sharp is the name of the key.

Duet in D

count (1   2) 3 4 &   1 & 2 & 3 (4   1) & 2 & 3 (4)

Dot over a note
means staccato

Play like this.   II Fine

Dynamic Etude (duet)

Etude #4

■ Be sure to hold all notes for their full value.

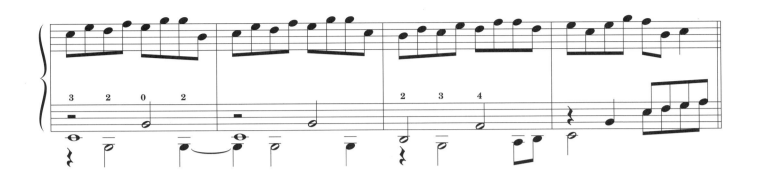

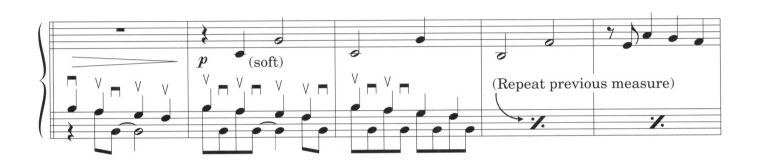

Key of A Major (First Position)
Duet in A

(All Fs, Cs, and Gs are sharped.)

Rhythm Accompaniment

■ **EXERCISE 1**

■ **EXERCISE 2**

56

Key of E♭ Major (Scale in First Position)

(All Bs, Es, and As are flatted.)

Duet in E♭

▐ Remember the flats. Count time carefully.

Moderate 4 (swing feeling)

57

Movable Chord Forms

A compilation of movable forms presented in Section I.

Related Fingerings

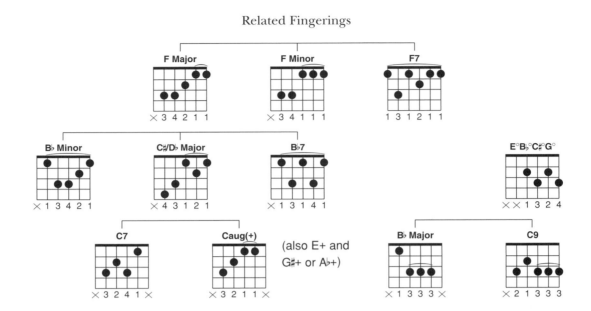

■ With these eleven forms, you can play the accompaniment to any song in any key, providing:
1. That you understand the principle of movable chord forms discussed on pg. 45, and
2. That you observe the following chart.

Chord Simplification and Substitution Chart

TYPE	WRITTEN					SIMPLIFIED SUBSTITUTION		
Major	C6	Cmaj7	Cmaj9	C^9_6	$Cmaj^9_7$	Use:	C major	
Dominant 7th	C9	C13	C9(11+)	C11+	———	Use:–	C7	
Dom 7-Altered 9th	C7(-9)	C7(♭9)	C13(-9)	C13(♭9)	———	—	C7 or G dim	{ build dim chord
	C7(+9)	C7(♯9)	C13(+9)	etc.	———	—	C7 (or G°)	on 5th note above C
Dom 7-Altered 5th	C7+	C7(+5)	Caug7	C9+	C9(+5) C+9	Use:	C+	{ build substitute
	C7(-5)	C7(♭5)	C9(-5)	etc. . .	$C7^{-5}_{+5}$ ——	—	C+ or G♭+	chord on flatted
Dom 7-Altered 5, 9	$C7^{-9}_{+5}$	$C7^{+9}_{+5}$	$C7^{+9}_{-5}$	$C7^{-9}_{-5}$	———	—	C+ or G♭7	5th above C
Dom 7-Sus 4	C7(sus4)	C7(susF)	C9(sus4)	C9(susF)	C11	Use:	G minor	5th note above C
Minor	Cm6	Cm^9_6				Use:	C minor	
Minor 7th	Cm7	Cm9	Cm11			Use:	Cm	
Min-with Maj7	Cm(♮7)	Cm(♯7)	Cm(maj7)			Use:	G+(5th above C) or Cm	
Min 7-Altered 5th	Cm7(-5)	Cm7(♭5)				Use:	E♭m	{ built on minor, (or lowered) 3rd above C

▌ Of course, having only eleven chord forms at your command will cause you to move up and down the fingerboard much more than is desired for good rhythm playing. The more forms you know, the less distance you have to travel and the more melodic your rhythm playing can become.

Picking—A Different Technique

The principle is to attack each new string with a downstroke.

This technique is older than alternate picking, and less emphasis is placed on it today. However it is one more step in right-hand control and, when mastered, it is very fast in ascending passages.

An example of this technique in use can be found on pg. 48, measure 20 of the "Endurance Etude." This type of picking will be suggested on the following pages from time to time *but only in certain situations* (arpeggios, whole tone scales, etc.) and only in addition to alternate picking. It will be up to you to gradually master and (whenever practical) add this style to your overall right-hand technique. However: the most concentrated effort must still be placed on alternate picking.

※ (>) Accent mark: strike more sharply

SECTION TWO
Position Playing

Position is determined by the fret on which the first finger plays. It is indicated by a Roman numeral. Strictly speaking, a position on the fingerboard occupies four adjacent frets. Some scales have one or more notes that fall outside this four-fret area, and these notes are to be played by reaching out with the first or fourth finger without shifting the entire hand, i.e. finger stretch or "FS." When the out-of-position note is a scale tone, the finger stretch is determined by the *fingering type* (Type I = first finger stretch, Type IV = fourth finger stretch). When the out-of-position note is not a scale tone and moving upward, use finger stretch 1, and moving downward finger stretch 4—regardless of fingering type. (All scale fingerings introduced from this point on will not use any open strings, and therefore they are movable in the same manner as the chord forms presented earlier. See pg. 45.)

Major Scales
C Major (Fingering Type 1)
Second Position

60

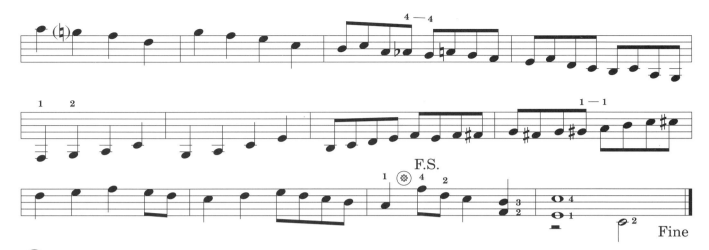

✺ When an out-of-position note is immediately preceded or followed by a note played with the same finger that would normally make the stretch, reverse the usual finger-stretch procedure. Always move back into a position from a finger stretch, never away from it.

EIGHTH-NOTE STUDY

ARPEGGIO STUDY: BROKEN CHORDS

❚ Practice picking as indicated and also with alternate ⊓∨ picking.

✺ ✺ When two consecutive notes are played with the same finger on adjacent strings, "roll" the finger tip from one string to the next. Do not lift the finger from the string.

Chord Etude No. 1

Practice slowly and evenly, connecting the chords so they flow from one to the next with no silences between them. Observe fingering and position marks!

Etude No. 5 (duet)

Remember, all natural notes on the guitar are two frets apart except E to F and B to C.

Reading Studies

Do not *practice* these two pages. Just read them, but not more than twice through during any single practice session. Do not play them on two consecutive days. Do not go back over any particular section because of a wrong note. Do keep an even tempo and play the proper time values.

By obeying these rules, you will never memorize the reading studies, so they will always be good reading practice. A little later on, it is recommended that you use this procedure with a variety of material, as this is the only way for a guitarist to achieve and maintain any proficiency in reading. (Even when working steadily, we are not reading every day, so "scare yourself" in the privacy of your practice sessions.)

C MAJOR 1 (FINGERING TYPE 1)

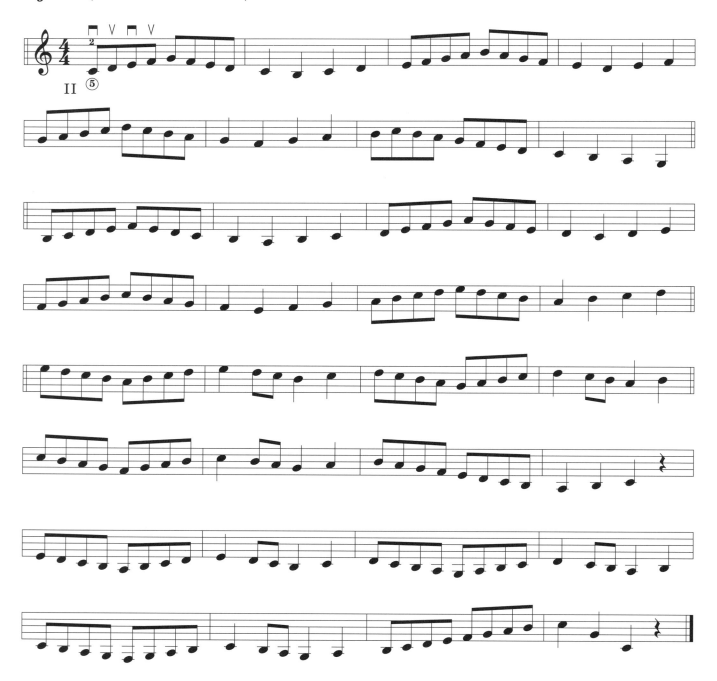

C MAJOR 2 (FINGERING TYPE 1)

Fine

If you encounter unusual difficulty reading these pages, go back to pg. 60 and start again.

Ballad (duet)

✻ A position mark in parentheses represents placement of second finger, as first finger is not used.

Movable Chord Forms
Rhythm Accompaniment, Part Two

The most difficult part of learning to play chords on the guitar is getting the fingers to fall instantly and without conscious effort in the proper arrangement on the fingerboard. This is mainly a physical problem, and a certain amount of practice time seems to be the only solution.

However, I have found that learning new chord forms in a certain order (a sequence of related fingerings) seems to lessen the time normally required to perform them.

Therefore, the following chord forms are presented in a particular order. We will use three of the previously learned fingerings as basic forms. We will alter these forms by moving, or removing, one or more fingers. In this way each new fingering is directly related to the one(s) preceding it.

So, each of the basic forms and each derivative is a preparation for another new chord form.

No specific letter names are given—only the chord type and the string on which the root is found.

Memorize the fingerings for all chord structures in their order of appearance. Do not skip around. Do not change the fingering of any form, even if you already play it in a different way. It will appear later on with "your" fingering, but related to a new set of forms. Practice all chord forms chromatically up and down the fingerboard, observing root (chord) names.

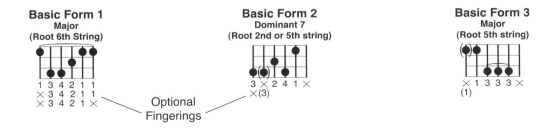

A dot in parentheses (•) means that although the note belongs to the chord, it need not sound and, in many cases, sounds better without it.

Chord Forms

Shown below is Basic Form 1 and seven derivative fingerings. When the basic form has been mastered, the performance of the derivatives is relatively easy to accomplish. Memorize the type of chord (major, minor, etc.) each form produces and the string on which the root (or name) is found. All optional fingerings should eventually be learned, but first concentrate on the one appearing directly below the diagram. It is the preferred one.

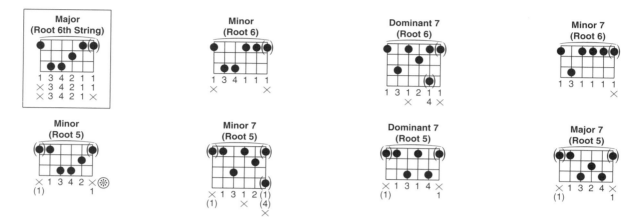

A word about notation:

1. When a chord is indicated by just a letter, it is major.
2. When it is a letter followed by a 7, it is a dominant 7 chord.
3. Minor is indicated by min, m, or a dash(—).
4. Major 7 is indicated by maj7, ma7, or sometimes M7.

■ EXERCISE

Use only the forms shown above. Watch the position marks!

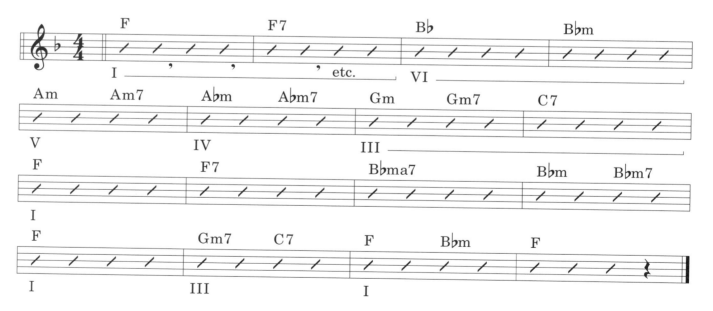

✸ The first string is not very effective in rhythm playing, and even when it is pressed down with a "barre" it is usually best to omit it by making the pick travel in an arc across the strings, passing above it. (⌒······)

Rhythm Accompaniment—Right-Hand Technique

To most beginners, strumming chords (pushing the pick across the strings so they sound one after the other) is easy and natural.

However, striking the chords so that the sound fits with a modern rhythm section is quite another thing, and requires considerable practice and know-how.

First, by using a combination rotary forearm and loose-wrist motion (snap the wrist as if flicking something from the back of your hand), you produce an explosive attack in which all notes seem to sound simultaneously.

Secondly, the placement of "pressure release points" (❜) and accents determines the types of beat produced. (Much more about all this later.)

Picking Etude No. 4
Observe fingering.

Hold third finger down throughout.

❀ *Grace note* to be played slightly before the top note G on the fourth beat.

F Major Scale
(Fingering Type 1A, Second Position)

The F major scale shown above is in the second position even though the first finger plays the first fret on three strings. This is because the three scale tones require stretches by the first finger. The basic four-fret position is never numbered from a stretch.

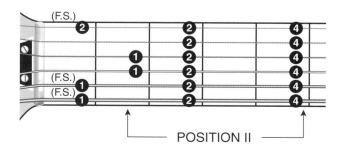

POSITION II

EIGHTH-NOTE STUDY

ARPEGGIO STUDY

Also practice arpeggios with alternate ⊓ ∨ picking, which is generally the most practical.

Chord Forms

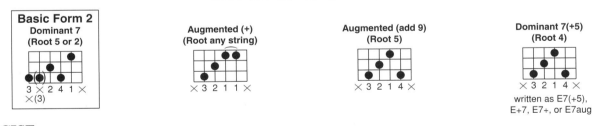

written as E7(+5),
E+7, E7+, or E7aug

■ EXERCISE
▌ Use the above forms plus some of the preceding ones.

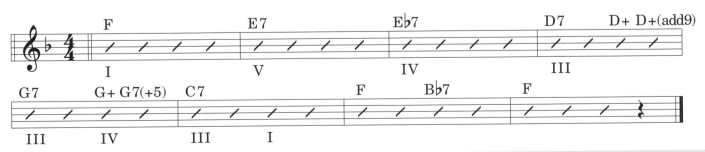

Transpose, write out, and practice all rhythm exercises in one or more higher keys.

Chord Etude No. 2

Rubato: Freedom of tempo. Accelerate and ritard as you wish.

These chord exercises are very important and should be reviewed *regularly*, as they serve many purposes, such as physical development of the left hand, fingering relationship between chord structures, and eventual "chord picture" recognition.

Another Duet in F

Regular review is a must!

Reading Studies

Just play these Reading Studies: Do not *practice* them, and do not play them on two consecutive days. (See pg. 64.)

F MAJOR 1 (FINGERING TYPE 1A)

F MAJOR 2 (FINGERING TYPE 1A)

FS: Finger Stretch. Stretch the finger; do not move the entire hand.

Play It Pretty (duet)

to coda ✛

to coda ✛

D.S. al coda

Repeat signs following a
D.S. or D.C. are not used. D.S. al coda

coda ✛ ✺

Ritard (poco a poco)

coda ✛

(III)

Fine

✺ A temporary change to position III at this point will simplify the fingering this passage, and eliminate the necessity of the open E (preceding the high B♭).

Chord Forms

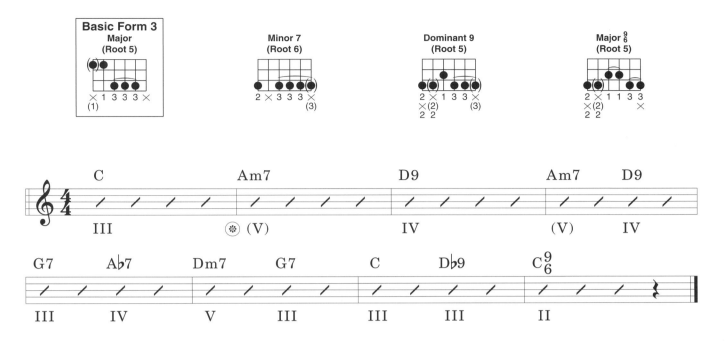

❀ A position mark in parentheses means that the first finger is omitted from the form. The position number is determined by the lowest fret used.

Triplet Study

Practice using both patterns of picking. See pg. 37.

Speed Study—Fingering Type 1

Maintain an even tempo. Play no faster than perfect coordination in both hands will allow. An increase in speed will come gradually.

Speed Study—Fingering Type 1A

■ Practice all speed studies as written and with a ♪♫ rhythm. Also play with and without repeats.

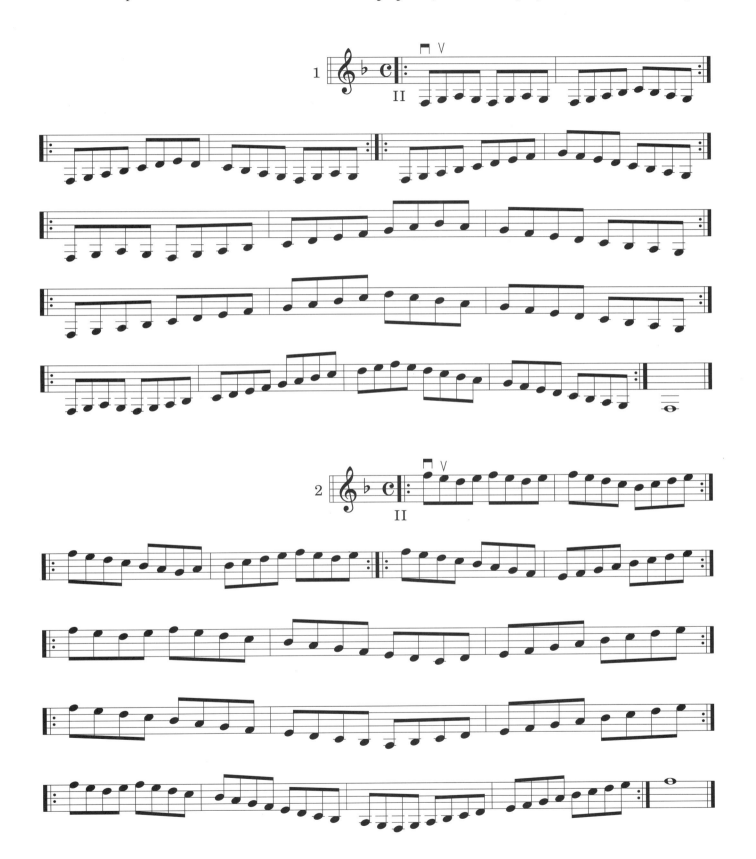

For additional technique-building patterns, see pg. 46.

G Major Scale
(Fingering Type 2, Second Position)

EIGHTH-NOTE STUDY

ARPEGGIO STUDY

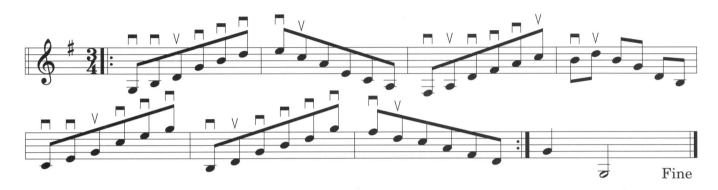

Also practice arpeggios with an alternate ⊓ V picking.

Dotted Eighth and Sixteenth Study

Practice as legitimate ♩. ♪ and as ♩₃♪ rhythms. See pg. 42.

When two consecutive notes on adjacent strings require the same finger, roll your finger; don't lift it.

Waltz for Two (duet)

⊕ coda

HARM. ✲

Ritard

⊕ coda

(XII)

Fine

✲ **Harmonic.** Lay the third finger lightly on the strings directly over the twelfth fret. Sharply strike the strings indicated, removing the third finger at almost the same instant. The resulting sound is in the same octave as notated (one octave above what you would expect to hear, as the guitar sounds one octave below the written note). These "natural" harmonics (from open strings) are also possible on other frets—the most practical being on the seventh and fifth frets.

Chord Forms

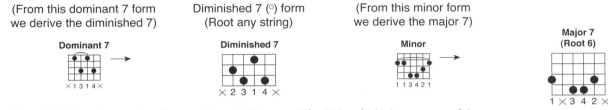

(From this dominant 7 form we derive the diminished 7)

Diminished 7 (°) form (Root any string)

(From this minor form we derive the major 7)

Major 7 (Root 6)

Dominant 7

× 1 3 1 4 ×

Diminished 7

× 2 3 1 4 ×

Minor

1 1 3 4 2 1

1 × 3 4 2 ×

 Diminished 7 chords are indicated by Gdim or G°. (The 7th is assumed.)

■ **EXERCISE 1**

Gmaj7 | G7 | Cma7 | Cm
III

Gma7 | A7 | D7 | F#° | G
III | V ———————— | III

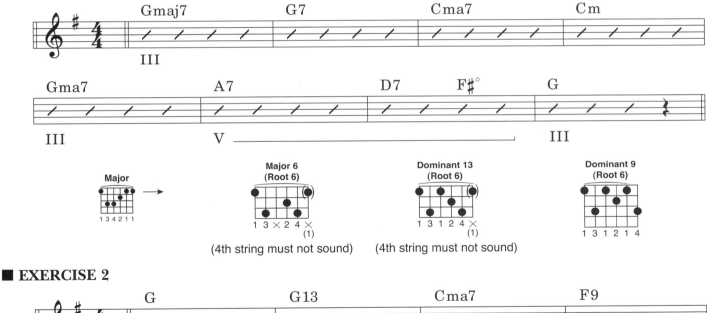

Major

1 3 4 2 1 1

Major 6 (Root 6)

1 3 × 2 4 ×
(1)
(4th string must not sound)

Dominant 13 (Root 6)

1 3 1 2 4
(1)
(4th string must not sound)

Dominant 9 (Root 6)

1 3 1 2 1 4

■ **EXERCISE 2**

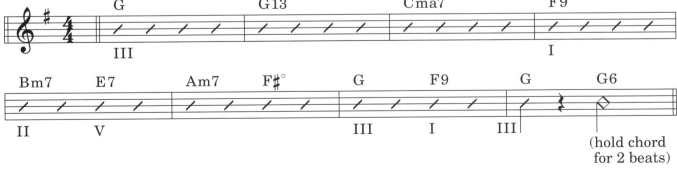

G | G13 | Cma7 | F9
III | | | I

Bm7 | E7 | Am7 | F#° | G | F9 | G | G6
II | V | | III | I | III
(hold chord for 2 beats)

■ You may substitute 6 and major 7 chords for major chords, and dominant 9 and 13 chords for dominant 7 chords.

Reading Studies

❚ Do not "practice" Reading Studies. Just read them.

G MAJOR 1 (FINGERING TYPE 2)

G MAJOR 2 (FINGERING TYPE 2)

❚ Continue on, without stopping, at the same tempo but in waltz time.

Fine

Speed not coming? Left-hand accuracy not consistent? Play any scale very slowly.
Watch your left hand. Force your fingers to remain poised over the fingerboard always in readiness.
Don't let them move too far away from the strings when not in use. Concentrate on this.

Blues in G (duet)

The 1st Guitar part of this duet is often played using the "muffled effect." This sound is produced by laying the right hand lightly along the top of the bridge. All strings being played must be kept covered. As this somewhat inhibits picking, the part should first be thoroughly practiced without the muffled effect (or "open").

For a different rhythm feel, play all consecutive eighth notes as a rhythm.

Chord Etude No. 3

■ Observe position marks and fingerings, as they will make possible a smooth performance.

When moving from chord to chord, the best fingering is usually the one
that involves the least motion in the left hand.
Leaving one finger free for possible melodic additions is also an important factor.

Rhythm Accompaniment—Right-Hand Technique

Memorize these symbols.

⊓   Downstroke

∨   Upstroke

(⸴)   Release finger pressure (of left hand) immediately *after* chord sounds. Do not remove from strings.

✕   Strike deadened strings (fingers in formation on strings, but no pressure).

>   Accent (strike sharply) with more force.

A basic Latin beat, which will work with the cha-cha, beguine, samba, and others.

Picking Etude No. 5

Hold down fourth finger throughout.

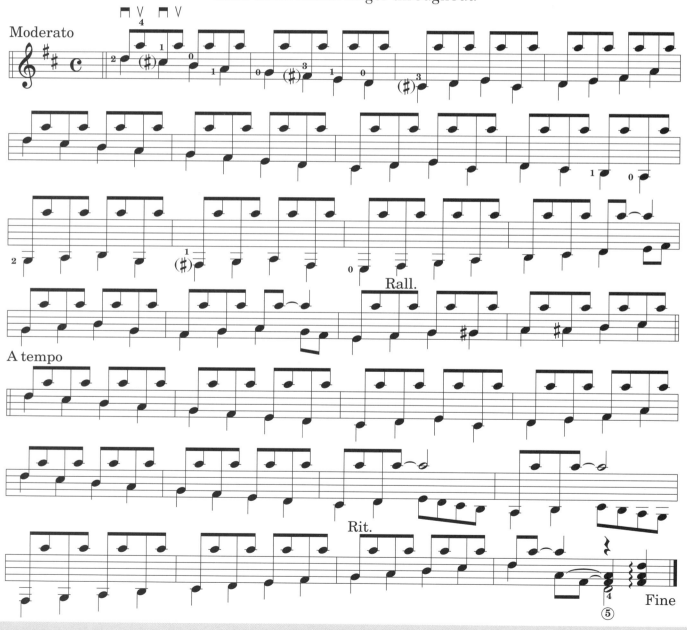

Review! Review!

Short and Sweet (duet)

D Major Scale
(Fingering Type 3, Second Position)

EIGHTH-NOTE STUDY

ARPEGGIO STUDY

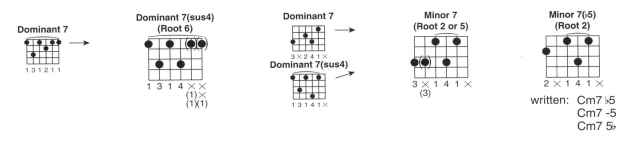

Also practice with alternate ⊓ ∨ picking.

Chord Forms

written: Cm7♭5
Cm7 -5
Cm7 5♭

■ EXERCISE

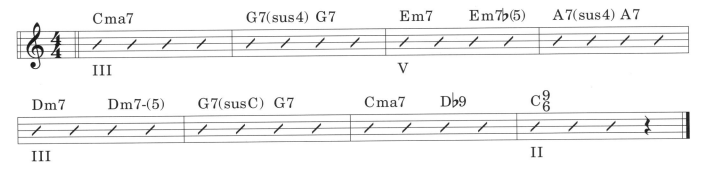

The sus4 refers to the 4th scale degree of the chord so named. The note name (for the 4th) is also used, e.g., G7susC. Sus4 may also be called (natural) 11. The root is on the same string as the sus4 form. For example, in the above exercise you may substitute symbols "G11" and "A11" for sus4.

Melodic Rhythm Study No. 1
Optional Duet With Rhythm Guitar

Be sure to count the rhythm until you can "feel" the phrase. Eventually you will be able to recognize (and feel) entire groups of syncopated notes. In the beginning you should pick *down* for notes falling on the beat, and *up* for those counted "and." This is a definite aid in learning to read these "off beat" rhythms. Later on, when syncopation is no longer a problem, you will vary your picking for the purpose of phrasing and accents.

❀ Rhythm Guitar: Use Latin beat.

❀ Rhythm Guitar _____ or _____. Remember the substitutions possible on the dominant 7 and major chords.

Chord Etude No. 4

Be sure to hold all notes for their full value.

Staccato, Legato

A dot (.) above or below a note means "staccato" or short.

A line (−) above or below a note means "legato" or long.

Reading Studies

For reading only.

D MAJOR 1 (FINGERING TYPE 3)

D MAJOR 2 (FINGERING TYPE 3)

Reading music is a combination of instant note (and finger) recognition and playing the "sound" that you "see" in music (along with the relative time durations of the notes, of course). Try this: Play the tonic chord of these reading studies to get your ear in the proper key. Then try to sing the music to yourself as you play it. If your fingers have been over the fingering type enough times, they will automatically play whatever notes (sound patterns) you mentally "hear" on the page. This will take a great deal of time to master, but keep after it. It's worth it!

Dee-Oo-Ett (duet)

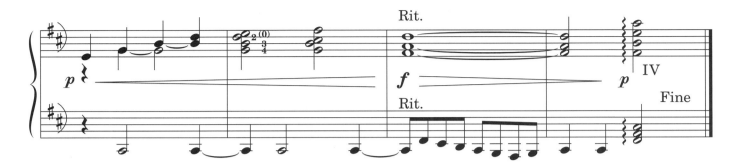

Chord Forms

■ EXERCISE

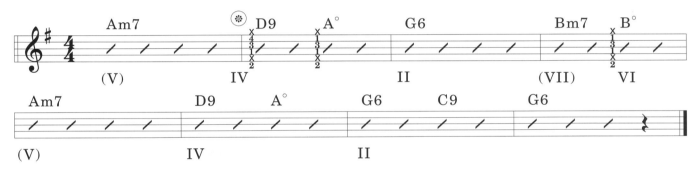

✿ The fingering will be given as shown here whenever two forms are possible in the same position (and also as an occasional reminder).

■ EXERCISE

❚ Latin beat—Be sure to release pressure where indicated (✖).

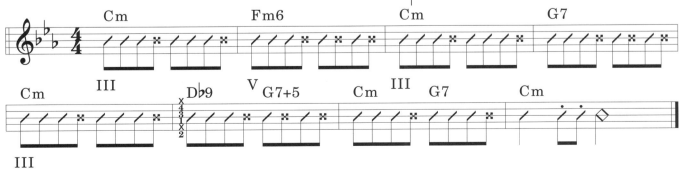

❚ The minor 6 form shown above may also be called a minor 7(♭5) (root 5th string).

Speed Study—Fingering Type 2

Maintain an *even tempo*. Play no faster than perfect coordination in both hands will allow. An increase in speed will come gradually.

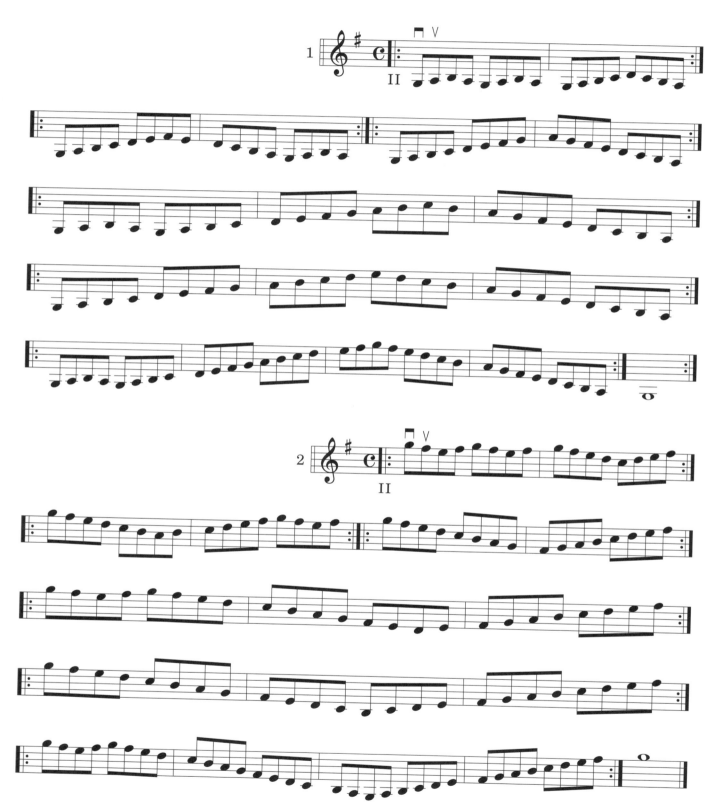

Speed Study—Fingering Type 3

Practice all speed studies as written and with ♪♫ rhythms. Also play them with and without repeats.

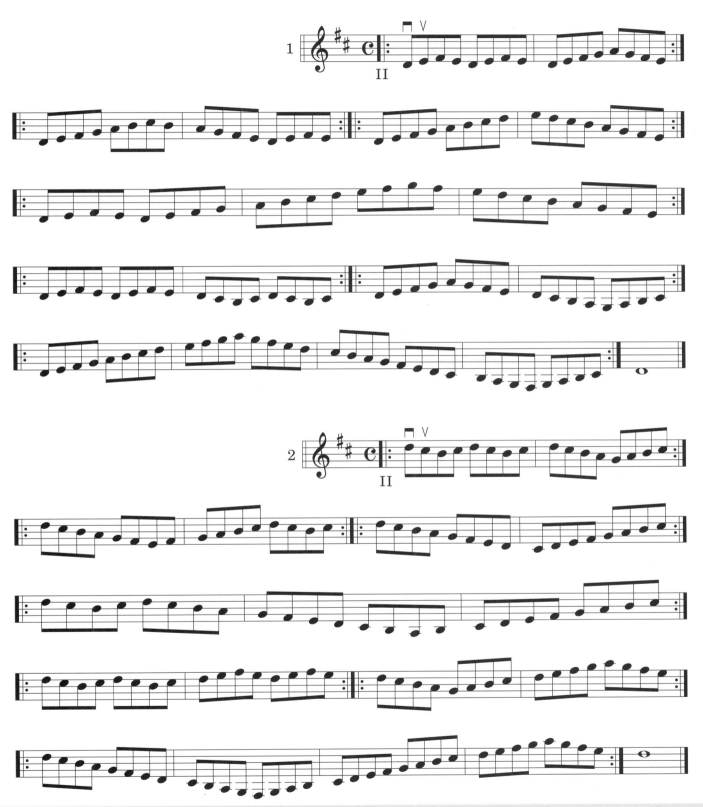

For additional technique-building patterns, see pg. 46.

A Major Scale
(Fingering Type 4, Second Position)

EIGHTH-NOTE STUDY

Cancellation reminder
(back to F♯, as in signature)

Double-sharp raises the
note one tone (two frets)

ARPEGGIO STUDY

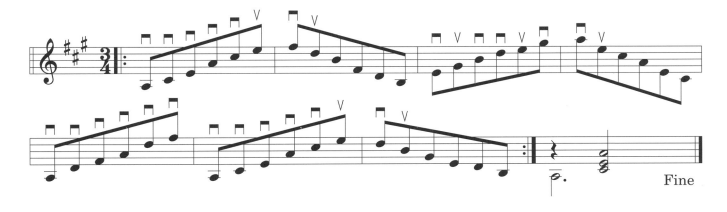

Fine

Also practice arpeggios with alternate ⊓ V picking.

Chord Etude No. 5

Fine

Reading Studies

▌ For reading only.

A MAJOR 1 (FINGERING TYPE 4)

A MAJOR 2 (FINGERING TYPE 4)

A MAJOR 3 (FINGERING TYPE 4)

Fine

Tres Sharp (duet)

Sixteenth Note Study

Count carefully. See pg. 31.

count 1 a & ah 2a & ah

1 a&ah 2a & ah 3 a &ah

Chord Forms

Minor 7

Major
(Root 2 or 5)

Dominant 7

Dominant 7 (sus4)
(Root 5)

(also called 11)

■ **EXERCISE**

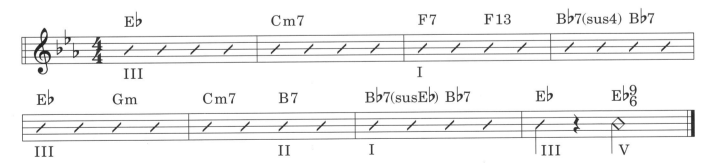

Speed Study—Fingering Type 4, Second Position

▌ As before, keep an even tempo. Play as written and with a ♪.♫ rhythm, with and without repeats.

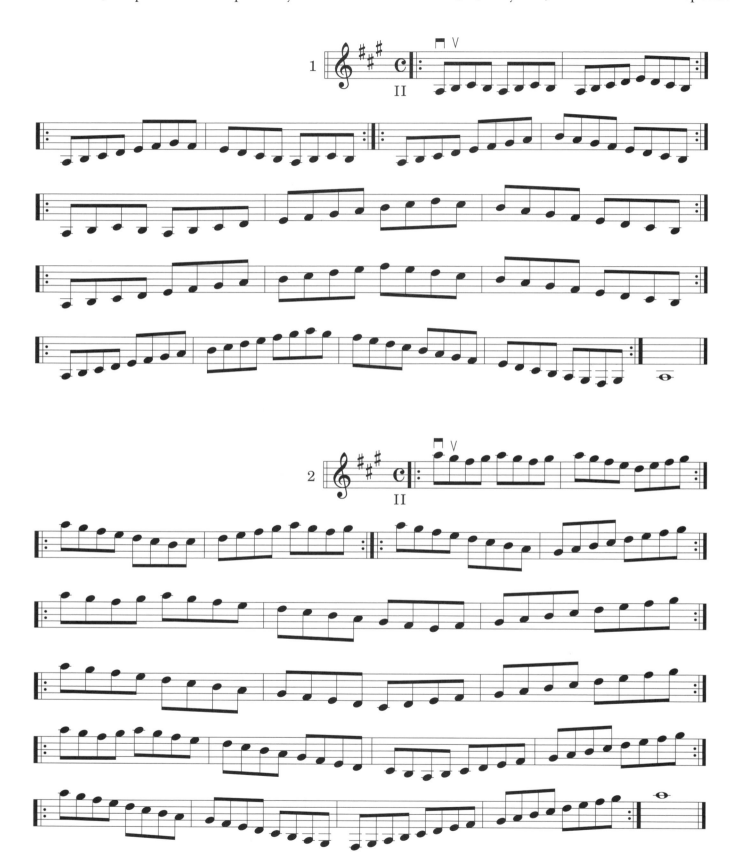

For additional technique-building patterns, see pg. 46.

Chord Forms

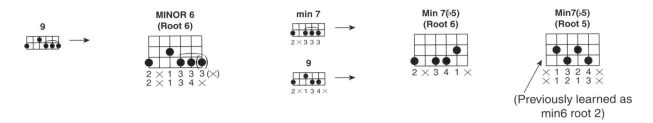

■ EXERCISE 1

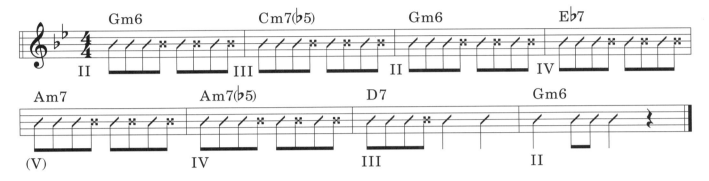

As the minor 6 and minor 7(♭5) forms tend to get confusing, study the following exercises, paying careful attention to the position marks. Play rhythm straight 4 (as written) and also practice using Latin beat. Experiment with various "pressure release" points to vary the accents.

■ EXERCISE 2

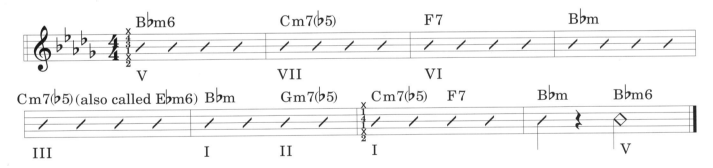

■ EXERCISE 3

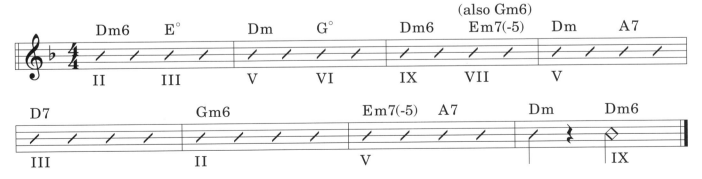

Transpose, write out, and practice all rhythm exercises one or more keys higher.

Second Position Review

Employing the five preceding major scales in position II.

When played as a duet:
- Melody guitar play as written; rhythm guitar play Latin beat.
- Melody guitar play consecutive eighth notes as ; rhythm guitar play straight 4.

FINGERING TYPE 1

Chord Forms

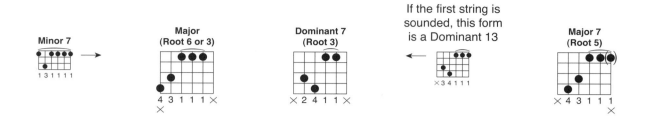

■ EXERCISE 1

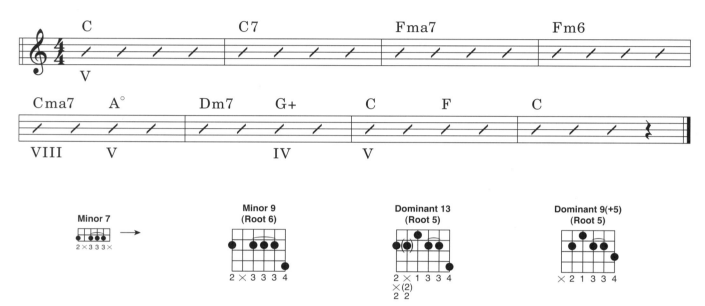

■ EXERCISE 2

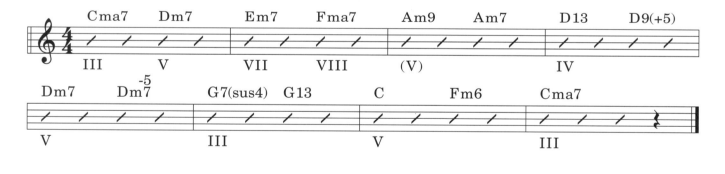

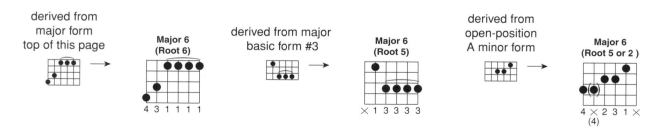

The third major 6 form shown here is, by far, the most valuable, as it does not use the first string, and therefore has a better rhythm sound.

Quarter-Note Triplets

Quarter-note triplets are very difficult to count. The most practical approach is to learn to "feel" them. This can be accomplished (as shown below) by playing two sets of eighth-note triplets using alternate picking and then two more sets of the same—but miss the string with the upstrokes of the pick.

Tap your foot while playing this exercise. Keep at it until you can "feel" the rhythm.

You are now able to read and play in five major keys in the second position. Actually, you can now play in five (major) keys in any position by using these same fingerings (Types 1, 1A, 2, 3, 4) on the higher frets.

Example: Position II major keys C, F, G, D, A

Position III C♯/D♭, F♯/G♭, A♭, E♭, B♭

Of course, you may not yet be able to read in these higher positions, as you have not seen the notes that correspond to these fingering patterns in any area of the fingerboard except the second position.
The following pages show the most used keys in the third position, first position (closed fingering, no open strings), and fourth position. You will be able to concentrate more on the notes, as by now, your fingers should know the patterns.

Major Scales in Third Position
(Most Used)

B-FLAT MAJOR (FINGERING TYPE 4)

E-FLAT MAJOR (FINGERING TYPE 3)

Fine

A-FLAT MAJOR (FINGERING TYPE 2)

Fine

D-FLAT MAJOR (FINGERING TYPE 1)

Double-flat lowers
note one tone

Cancellation
reminder–back to
B♭ as in signature

Fine

Third Position Review
Optional Duet With Rhythm Guitar
Employing the four preceding major scales in position III.

▌ When played as a duet:
- Melody guitar as written; rhythm guitar with optional Latin beat.
- Melody guitar play consecutive eighth notes as a ♩♪ rhythm; rhythm guitar play straight 4.

TYPE 4

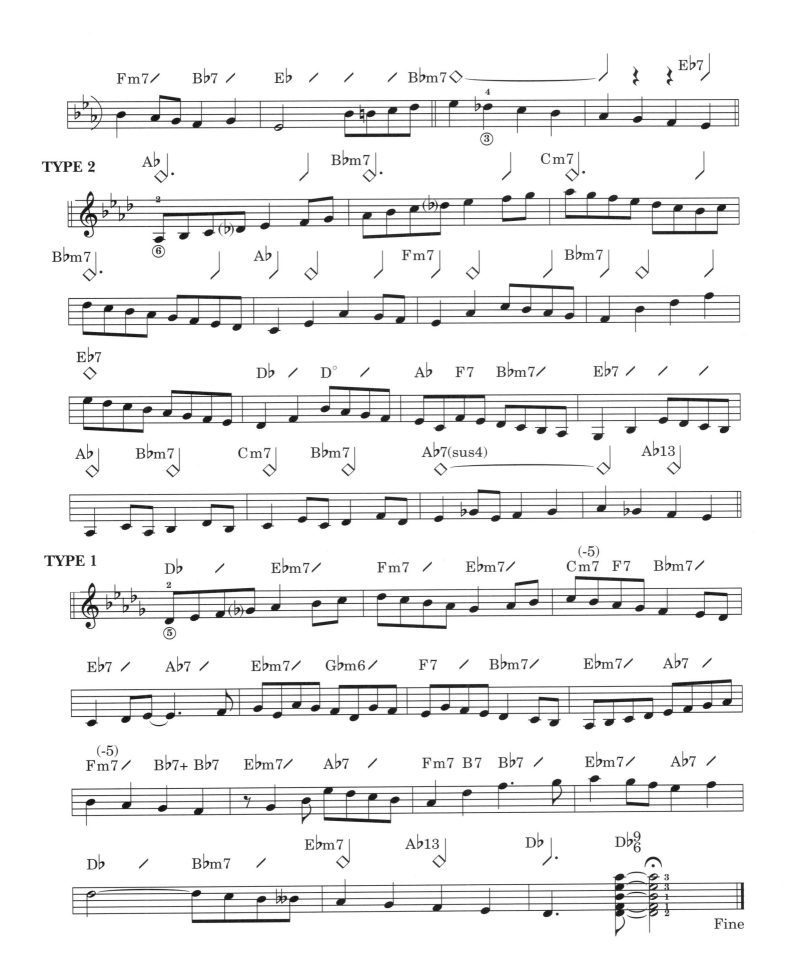

Chord Forms

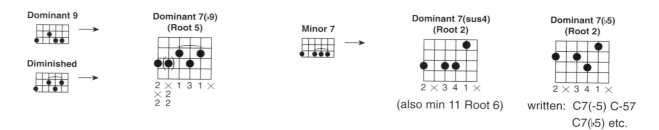

■ **EXERCISE 1**

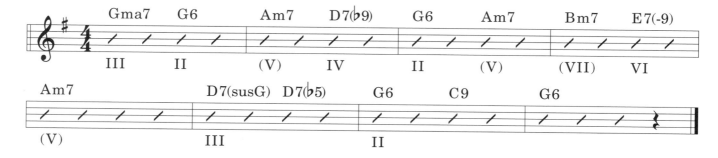

(The dominant 7(♭5) form shown above may also be named from the 6th string.)

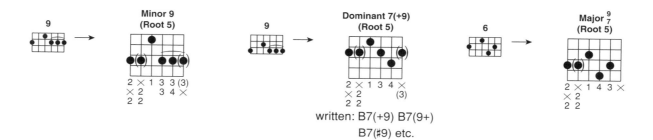

■ **EXERCISE 2**

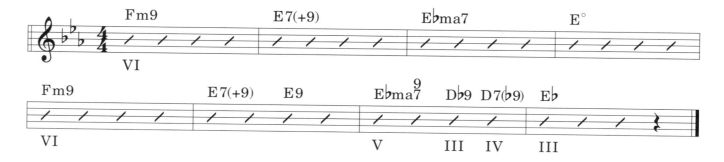

The E7(+9) chord used above would be called: E7(♯9), E7 raise 9, or E7 augmented 9. This explicit reference to the altered degree is important.

Major Scales in First Position
(Most Used)
No open strings.

A-FLAT MAJOR (FINGERING TYPE 4)

Fine

D-FLAT MAJOR (FINGERING TYPE 3)

Fine

First Position Review
Optional Duet With Rhythm Guitar
Employing the two preceding major scales in position I.

Melody guitar plays consecutive eighth notes as written and as ♪ rhythms. Rhythm guitar plays a waltz beat ♪ ♪ ♪ for both types of eighth-note rhythms.

Major Scales in Fourth Position
(Most Used)

G MAJOR (FINGERING TYPE 1A)

Fine

D MAJOR (FINGERING TYPE 1)

Fine

A MAJOR (FINGERING TYPE 2)

Fine

E MAJOR (FINGERING TYPE 3)

Fine

Chord Forms

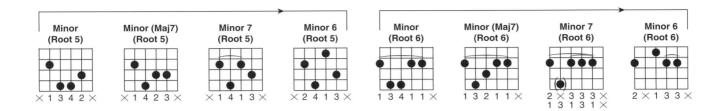

■ EXERCISE 1

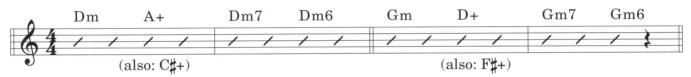

These same minor chord sequences are often found written like this:

■ EXERCISE 2

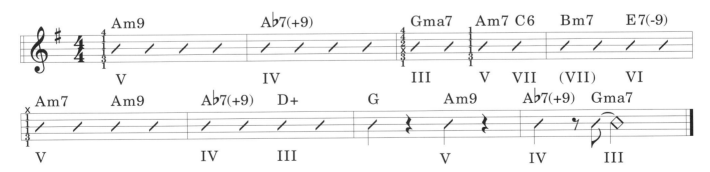

Substitution Tip: ♭5 and ♯5 forms are almost always interchangeable (also +9 and ♭9).

Fourth Position Review
Optional Duet With Rhythm Guitar
Employing the two preceding major scales in position IV.

Melody guitar plays consecutive eighth notes as written and as ♩₃♪ rhythm. Rhythm guitar plays a waltz beat for both types of eighth-note rhythms.

TYPE 2

TYPE 3

Fine

Find additional reading material. *Be sure it is easy to execute.* Then read five or more pages every day. Play each page *not more* than twice through. Do not practice, do not memorize, and do not use the same pages on consecutive days. Vary the material, and READ, READ, READ, READ.

Chord Forms

The root of this form is one fret below any fingered note. It has four possible names, like the diminished 7 chord.

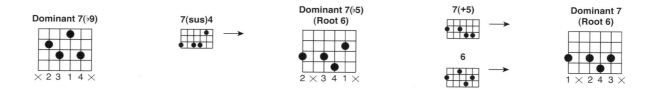

■ EXERCISE

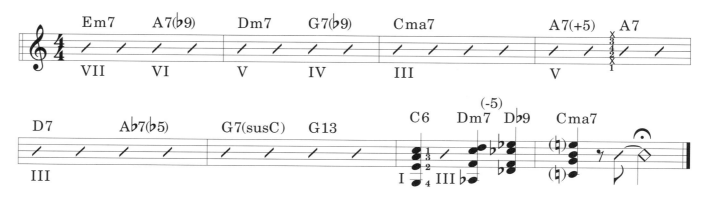

Author's Notes

All forms presented in this book that employ the 6th string (and therefore sound in part in the real bass register) have the root (first) or fifth chordal degrees sounding on the bottom. These are the "strongest" chord tones and *always sound right.*

You have probably seen some of these same forms elsewhere with different chord names indicated. Theoretically, these other names are also correct. However, the bass notes are "weak" chordal degrees and require special handling. This will be discussed thoroughly in a later section. Until then be careful of any forms that use the 6th string and do not have the root or fifth in the bass as they do not always sound right.

In an orchestral rhythm part, the chord symbols used generally indicate the total or complete harmonic structures, and it is not expected (nor is it possible) that you play all degrees at all times. Of course, you should try to play as close as possible to the written sequences. Actually, simplification by omitting some of the chordal degrees is the "norm." (It is best, for now, to omit the higher degrees.)

Examples: For C7+5($\flat$9) you may play: C7(+5) (omit the $\flat$9) or C+
For G7 ($\flat$9,13) you may play: G7($\flat$9) (omit the 13) or G7
For F9(sus4) you may play: F7(sus4) (omit the 9)

Be very careful of substitutions, as they must be completely compatible with the chord(s) indicated. (More about this in later volumes.)

Now, in addition to the five major keys in the second position, you should be somewhat familiar with the most used major scales in positions I, III, and IV. You will have to do a great deal of reading in these areas, however, to really know them.

I cannot overemphasize the importance of learning the four major scale fingering types well, as they are the foundation for other kinds of scales. We will gradually add more (major) fingering patterns until, ultimately, we have twelve—one for each key in each position. At the same time, we will learn how to *convert previously practiced* major forms onto jazz minor, harmonic minor, etc.

Our next project (*Modern Method for Guitar, Volume II*) will be to learn the notes on the entire fingerboard by using all fingering types *in the same key.* This will require moving from position to position as we go through the patterns. The sequence of patterns will vary, depending upon the key signature. You will have a definite advantage in learning the fingerboard in this manner, as your fingers "know" the patterns and you can concentrate on the notes.

Remember, learning to play the guitar is an accumulative process. Regular, complete review is absolutely necessary for the gradual improvement and perfection of the techniques.

Index